EXPLORATION THROUGH THE AGES

THE VOYAGES OF CAPTAIN COOK

Richard Humble

Illustrated by
Richard Hook

Franklin Watts
New York · London · Toronto · Sydney

Franklin Watts Inc
387 Park Avenue South
New York, N.Y. 10016

Library of Congress Cataloging-in-Publication Data

Humble, Richard.
    The voyages of Captain
Cook/Richard Humble.
    p. cm — (Exploration through the ages)
    Summary: Examines the training and accomplishments of Captain James Cook and reconstructs his explorations and journeys to Hawaii, New Zealand, and Australia.
    ISBN 0-531-14066-0
    1. Cook, James. 1728–1799 — Journeys — Juvenile literature. 2. Voyages around the world — Juvenile literature. 3. Explorers — Great Britain — Biography — Juvenile literature. [1. Cook, James, 1728–1799. 2. Explorers. 3. Voyages around the world.]
    I. Title. II. Series.
    G420.C73H86 1990
    910'.92—dc20   90-12173
    [B]   CIP
    [92]   AC

Designer: Ben White
Series editor: Deborah Fox
Editor: Sally Jordan
Picture researcher: Sarah Ridley
Illustrations: Richard Hook,
Hayward Art Group
Consultants: John Robottom, and
Margarette Lincoln.

Photographs: John Lancaster 9; National Maritime Museum, London 4, 22, 24, 26, 28l, 28r, 29bl, 29br; By courtesy of the Natural History Museum, London 21, 29t; Public Records Office London (Adm 1/1612 – MPl83) 22.

Words in bold appear in the glossary.

Printed in Belgium

Contents

Search for a southern land 4
The making of a sea captain 6
HMS Endeavour 8
Off Cape Horn 10
The Transit of Venus 12
Charting New Zealand's coasts 14
Surviving the Barrier Reef 16
In Antarctic seas 18
Worshipped as a god 20
Off Alaska's coast 22
Return to Hawaii 24
Death of a great explorer 26
The legacy of Captain Cook 28
Glossary 30
Timechart 31
Index 32

Search for a southern land

Less than 250 years ago, nearly half the surface of the Earth still lay blank on the maps of the world. The **hemisphere** of the great land continents – Europe and Asia, Africa, and the Americas – was well enough known to the world's mapmakers. But next to nothing was known about the hemisphere of water dominated by the greatest ocean on Earth: the Pacific.

The first European sailors to cross the Pacific had been those led by Ferdinand Magellan of Portugal on the first voyage around the world in 1519–21. They had been followed by others from Spain, Holland, France, and Britain. These explorers had found many new lands in the vastness of the Pacific: lush tropical islands, and strange patches of coast which might, some day, prove to be joined together in a huge southern continent.

This became known in Europe as *Terra Australis Incognita* – the "unknown southern land."

But the distances involved were so great, and the science of ocean **navigation** still so primitive, that many of these early discoveries could not be found again by later voyages. The first ocean voyagers only had crude navigating instruments and so the positions of the new lands they

▽ A French world map of 1755 shows the earlier Dutch discoveries of New Holland, Van Diemen's Land, and New Zealand (right). Were these all part of a huge southern continent?

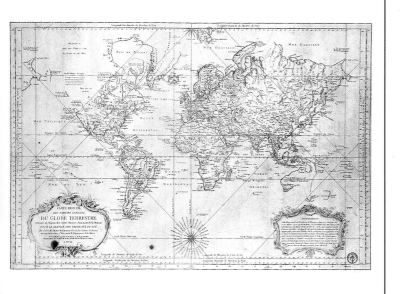

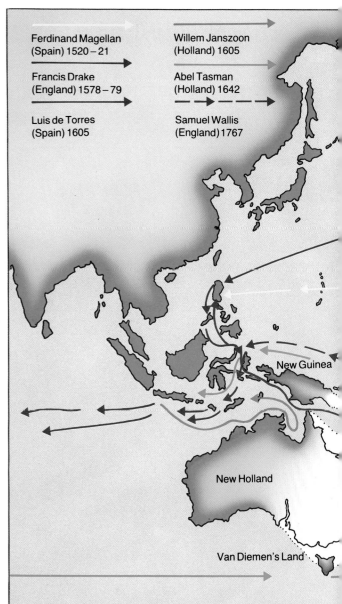

Ferdinand Magellan
(Spain) 1520 – 21

Francis Drake
(England) 1578 – 79

Luis de Torres
(Spain) 1605

Willem Janszoon
(Holland) 1605

Abel Tasman
(Holland) 1642

Samuel Wallis
(England) 1767

New Guinea

New Holland

Van Diemen's Land

recorded were often hundreds of miles in error. These lands did not offer anything like the fortunes to be made by exploiting the known riches of Africa, the Americas, and Asia.

After the famous voyage of Magellan, nearly 250 years passed before the Pacific Ocean began to be properly explored – by sailors sent to find scientific knowledge rather than easy money and plunder.

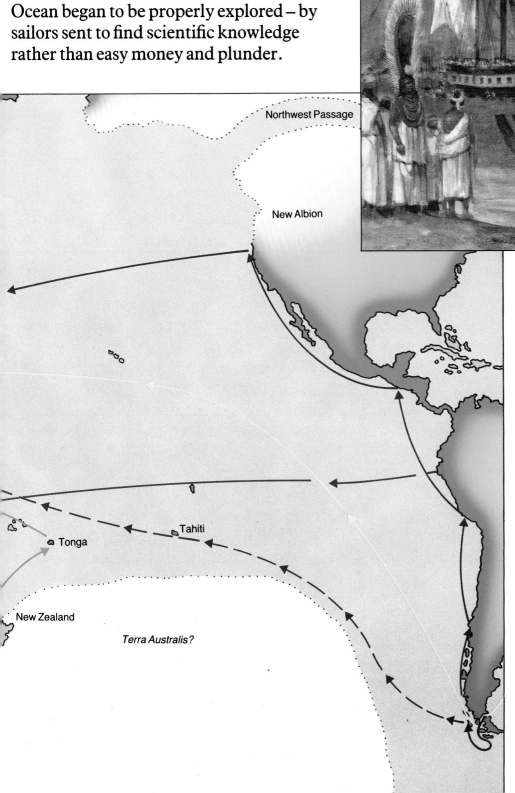

Northwest Passage

New Albion

Tonga

Tahiti

New Zealand

Terra Australis?

▽ Tahitian islanders row out with gifts for the French explorers led by the Chevalier de Bougainville in 1768. By the late 1760s growing interest in the Pacific by Britain's rival, France, was encouraging the British to make greater efforts of their own and not be left behind.

◁ Voyages and discoveries in the South Pacific between the discovery of New Guinea by the Spaniards, Quiros and Torres, in 1605–6, and the discovery of Tahiti by the Englishman, Wallis, in 1767. The latter was the prelude to the first voyage of James Cook in 1768.

5

The making of a sea captain

James Cook was the second of eight children and was born in the Yorkshire village of Marton-in-Cleveland on October 27, 1728. His family had nothing to do with the sea, nor had he any important relatives to encourage or help him in a seagoing career.

Cook's father was a farm laborer who worked his way up to become a farm manager and saw to it that James was taught to read and write. In an age when there were no free schools for the poor, James was encouraged to learn all he could and make a better life for himself than working on a farm.

When James was seventeen he moved to the nearby fishing port of Staithes to work in the shop of William Sanderson, but after eighteen months he decided that he would prefer a life at sea to one in a shop. Sanderson generously took James to the busy port of Whitby and arranged for him to become an apprentice to John Walker, an important Whitby shipowner and coal shipper.

Over the next ten years James Cook became a tough and experienced seaman on the east coast shipping route, sailing between the coal ports of northern England and London. He learned the vicious moods of the North Sea, and how to steer ships along often dangerous coasts. Between voyages he lived in Walker's house. At these times he learned all he could about the science of navigation from books relating this to his experience afloat.

Cook rose steadily from apprentice to able seaman, and on to mate. In summer 1755, Walker offered Cook the command of his ship *Friendship*. It was a splendid opportunity – but Cook astonished Walker by turning it down. He had chosen a new career, joining the Royal Navy as a volunteer seaman.

In the Navy, Cook's ability to learn fast and work hard earned him rapid promotion. By 1758 he had risen from able seaman to the highly important rank of master. This meant he was responsible to the captain for the navigation, sailing, and smooth running of the ship. His Navy career was greatly helped by the Seven Years War of 1756–63. As master of HMS *Pembroke*, Cook plotted the course up the St. Lawrence River that enabled the British fleet to take Quebec, Canada. The fleet landed the army there, where they were to defeat the French. Cook's excellent chart of the St. Lawrence was still being used 100 years later.

Between 1763 and 1768 Cook worked hard at charting the coast of Labrador and Newfoundland. In August 1766 he made detailed observations of a total eclipse of the sun; these were highly valued by the scientists of the Royal Society in London.

In 1768 the Society asked the Navy to provide a ship to sail to the Pacific island of Tahiti to observe a very rare event: the transit of the planet Venus across the sun. Because of his experience as a mapmaker and observer, James Cook was chosen to command the expedition. He was then 40 years old.

▷ The 27-year-old James Cook tells his employer, Whitby shipowner, John Walker, that he is determined to join the Royal Navy. In the background lies a Whitby "cat," one of the sturdy coal ships in which Cook learned the seaman's trade between 1746 and 1755.

HMS Endeavour

The vessel chosen for the Tahiti expedition of 1768 is the earliest ship used for discovery for which accurate details are known. Not surprisingly, Cook recommended the type of ship he knew well. It was a North Sea coal "cat," the *Earl of Pembroke*, renamed HMS *Endeavour* after her transfer to the Navy.

Whitby coal cats were tough and broad in the beam, with a straight **keel** on which they were designed to sit upright when grounded between tides. Though the Navy was not used to buying or hiring such ships, the surveyors who chose *Endeavour* pointed out that cats were ideal for long voyages—"their kind are roomly and will afford the advantage of stowing and carrying a large quantity of provisions, so necessary on such voyages."

Endeavour was given an extra deck in her big cargo hold, and square ports were

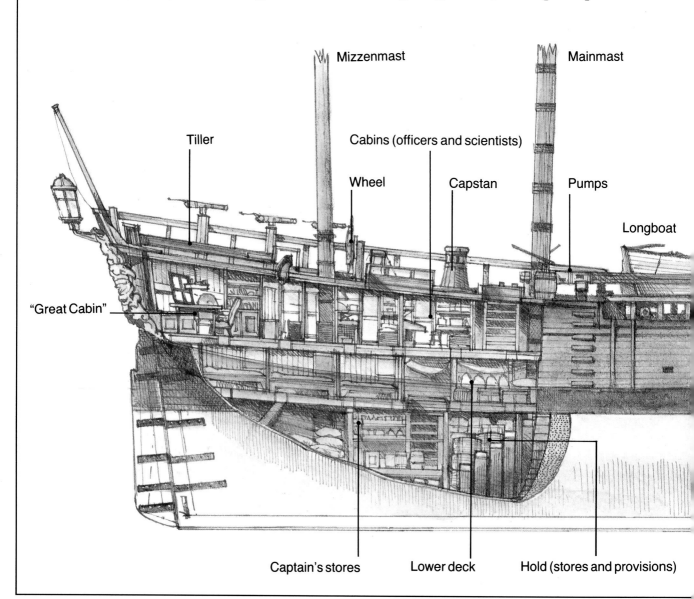

Mizzenmast

Mainmast

Tiller

Cabins (officers and scientists)

Wheel

Capstan

Pumps

Longboat

"Great Cabin"

Captain's stores

Lower deck

Hold (stores and provisions)

△ The sturdy timber frame and broad lines of Cook's *Endeavour,* taking shape in a rebuilding of the ship in Fremantle, western Australia, to honor the 200th anniversary of the Australian nation.

▽ Cutaway view of HMS *Endeavour,* showing the extra lower deck built across the former cargo hold. Much of the limited cabin space went to the **natural scientists, astronomers** and artists on board.

cut in her sides for the mounting of ten guns on carriages. As protection against the worms of the tropic seas that could riddle a wooden ship with underwater holes, the underside of her hull was given an extra shell of oak planks, secured with flat-headed nails driven in close together. (In future years ships were protected with sheets of copper.)

Endeavour's keel length was 24.7 meters (81 ft), and her greatest width or beam was 8.9 meters (29 ft 2 in). She carried five anchors, three boats, a total of 94 men including officers, scientists, servants and crewmen.

▽ *Endeavour's* sail plan. The lower sails were the "courses," the middle ones "topsails," and the upper ones the "topgallants." The **yards** supporting the sails could be lengthened with extension **booms** to carry extra sails known as "studding sails," which gave more speed when winds were favorable.

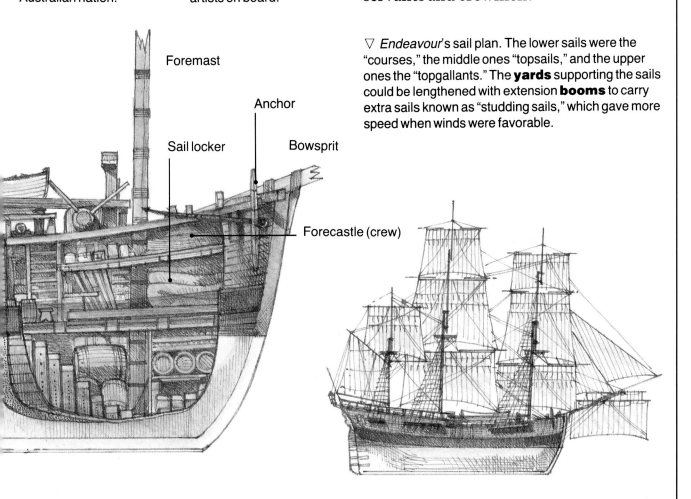

Foremast

Anchor

Sail locker

Bowsprit

Forecastle (crew)

Off Cape Horn

When *Endeavour* sailed for the Pacific from Plymouth on August 25, 1768, Cook had never sailed south of the **equator** before. But he was able to use much useful knowledge gained by others on earlier long-distance voyages, and this knowledge greatly added to his chances of success.

It was known, for example, that the worst killer disease on long ocean voyages was scurvy, caused by a poor diet. In 1741 the three ships of Commodore George Anson had lost 626 men out of 961 on a nightmare voyage into the Pacific, nearly all killed by scurvy.

Cook's expedition of 1768 carried a variety of new foods to fight scurvy: pickled cabbage, concentrated orange and lemon juice, malt extract and blocks of marrow-stock "portable soup" to vary the basic Navy rations of salt meat, hard biscuit and rum. Also, to set standards of cleanliness, Cook ventilated the lower decks daily and ordered that clothing, hammocks and blankets should be aired on deck. These measures were not always popular, but the men could appreciate Cook's concern for their welfare.

Other vital knowledge available to Cook concerned the violent storms which, blowing from west to east, could cause terrible damage to ships trying to round Cape Horn from the Atlantic into the Pacific. Anson's ships, trying to round the Horn in April, had been battered nearly to wrecks. By 1768 it was known that the best months for tackling Cape Horn were December and January – never after March.

After stopping at Madeira for fresh provisions – wine and water – *Endeavour* crossed the equator on October 25 and reached Rio de Janeiro on November 13. After taking on more supplies, Cook headed south on December 7 for the long approach of 3,220 km (2,000 mi) to Tierra del Fuego, which was sighted on January 11, 1769. With *Endeavour's* **studding sails** set, Cook passed Cape Horn – "an island with a very high round hummock upon it" – in fair weather, and headed into the Pacific Ocean on January 30.

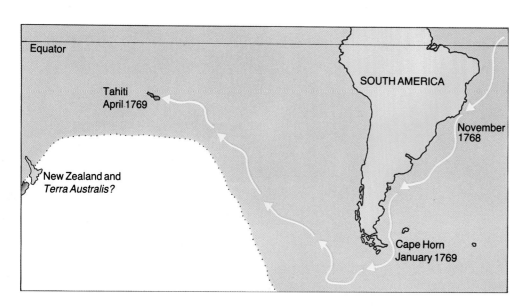

Equator

Tahiti
April 1769

New Zealand and
Terra Australis?

SOUTH AMERICA

November
1768

Cape Horn
January 1769

◁ Cook's course from Plymouth to Tahiti, with the rounding of Cape Horn ("thought by some to be a mighty thing," as he wrote) made at the best season of the year.

▷ With *Endeavour* in sight of the ominous hummock of Cape Horn, Cook and astronomer Charles Green take accurate sightings to confirm the ship's true position.

The Transit of Venus

On April 13, 1769 *Endeavour* dropped anchor in Matavai Bay, Tahiti, and the first stage of her voyage was over. It was a remarkable achievement for Cook, considering that this was his first long ocean voyage.

On his approach to Tahiti, Cook had chosen to cross the Pacific further south than any voyager before him, proving that if *Terra Australis* did exist, it must lie further to the west than had been believed.

Endeavour's crew and her scientist passengers were in good health. Cook had lost four men through accidents and one by suicide (a man accused of theft), but none from scurvy or other sickness. Most captains of the day would have thought this little less than a miracle. And though advised to try and reach Tahiti six weeks before the date of the Transit of Venus (June 3), Cook had done it with seven weeks and one day to spare.

The Transit of Venus was a very rare event. After 1769, it would not occur again until 1874, 1882, 2004 and 2012. The Royal Society wanted the 1769 transit to be observed in as many places as possible, using the same clocks so that the results could be carefully compared.

Cook's first concern was to establish friendly relations with the Tahitian chiefs, Tupia and Tutaha. He ordered *Endeavour*'s crewmen to deal fairly with the Tahitians by trading honestly for food and native goods. But Cook was anxious about the safety of the astronomical equipment and so he built a fort at "Point Venus" within which the observatory to watch the transit was set up.

On June 3, in a cloudless sky, "the whole of the passage of the Planet Venus over the Suns disk" was observed by Cook, astronomer Charles Green, and **botanist** Daniel Carl Solander. Their mission was accomplished – and yet the greatest discoveries of the voyage still lay ahead.

◁ In the blazing heat of a perfect Tahitian day, Cook and his fellow observers at "Fort Venus" watch the historic transit. "We very distinctly saw an atmosphere or dusky shade around the body of the Planet," noted Cook.

Charting New Zealand's coasts

After observing the Transit of Venus, Cook was under orders to head south. If he failed to find the elusive *Terra Australis* he was to explore New Zealand, Tasman's discovery of 1642, before turning for home.

Cook sailed from Tahiti on July 13, 1769 with a new passenger: the Tahitian Tupia, who had offered to sail back to England in *Endeavour*. Tupia proved very useful as a guide and interpreter during the month Cook spent cruising among the islands west of Tahiti, before turning south on August 9.

By September 1 Cook had sailed 40° south of the equator without finding a trace of *Terra Australis*, so he turned north again. At the beginning of October, ship's boy Nicholas Young sighted land to the

west. Cook kept his promise to the crew and named the landfall after the successful lookout: Young Nick's Head, north of Hawke Bay.

Endeavour had clearly reached the eastern coast of Tasman's New Zealand, but the first encounter proved that the native New Zealanders were very different from the friendly Tahitians. A fierce and proud warrior race, the Maoris of New Zealand distrusted the strangers from the sea and repeatedly attacked them. War canoes manned by Maori warriors often had to be kept at bay as Cook began the exploration of New Zealand's coasts, though other Maoris proved friendly and willing to trade.

It took nearly six months for Cook to complete the first voyage around New

▷ Maori warriors yell defiance as *Endeavour* cruises warily off the New Zealand coast. Not surprisingly, on the other side of the world with no hope of rescue, Cook's men remained constantly alert against attacks.

Zealand. He proved that New Zealand was not one island, but two—and not, as had been previously believed, the long extension of a southern continent. Having completed the world's first map or chart of New Zealand, Cook had carried out his orders and sailed to the west on March 31, 1770. With New Zealand behind her, *Endeavour* now headed for the unknown perils of the dangerous coral-fringed coast of "New Holland."

Surviving the Barrier Reef

When he sailed west from New Zealand, Cook intended to return home by way of the Dutch East Indies (modern Indonesia). First, however, he wanted to find and explore the eastern coast of "New Holland": the huge island landmass first sighted by the Dutch over 100 years before. The result was a voyage that produced the first accurate map of what we now call the east coast of Australia – but which came close to ending in shipwreck and disaster.

The new land to the west was sighted 19 days out from New Zealand. Cook was surprised that it lay well north of the reported position of "Van Diemen's Land," the southernmost point of "New Holland" sighted by Tasman in 1642. (He could not know that "Van Diemen's Land" was really the island of Tasmania, separated from Australia by the wide Bass Strait.) But he set off to follow and map the new coast stretching away to the north.

Cook sailed slowly along the coast of

New South Wales, naming and mapping the anchorages of Botany Bay and the future Sydney Harbor. Botany Bay was so named because of the large number of new plants the botanist and naturalist on board collected in this place. By the beginning of June 1770, *Endeavour* was now entering the dangerous maze of shallows and sharp coral formed by the huge Great Barrier Reef, over 19,300 km (1,200 mi) long.

Despite *Endeavour*'s slow speed, careful lookouts and constant **sounding** to check the depth of water, she crashed into the Barrier Reef on the night of June 11, 1770. Hard work refloated her and a sail was stretched over the hole to stop her from sinking, though there was nothing to do but run *Endeavour* ashore in order to make proper repairs.

Once beached, she was emptied of guns and supplies and "careened," or heeled over, to expose the damaged planking. During the next few weeks the crew camped ashore, foraging for fruit and vegetables and shooting kangaroos for their meat.

By the first week of August 1770, repairs were completed and Cook set off again, carefully following the coast of Cape York north to the dangerous Torres Straits between Australia and New Guinea. After making more repairs at Java in the East Indies, Cook headed across the Indian Ocean for the Cape of Good Hope and the Atlantic, with "Young Nick" sighting the coast of England on July 10, 1771.

◁ Emptied of supplies and kept firmly heeled over by a cannon slung from her main **yardarm**, *Endeavour* undergoes repairs after her near fatal grounding on the Great Barrier Reef. In the foreground a hunting party hungry for fresh meat chases a group of kangaroos, formerly unknown to Europeans.

In Antarctic seas

There was much excitement over the discoveries made by Cook in *Endeavour*. He was congratulated by King George III, and promoted to the rank of commander. But there was almost more interest in what Cook had *not* discovered than in what he had, and he was soon ordered to prepare for a second voyage.

Cook suggested another search for *Terra Australis,* but this time further south than had ever been tried before: south of **Latitude** 40°, over 4,800 km (3,000 mi)

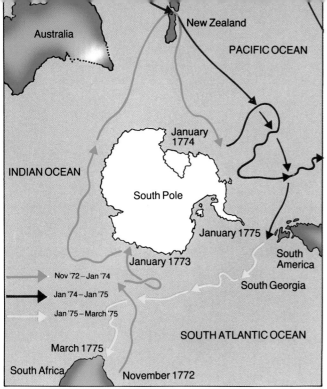

Australia
New Zealand
PACIFIC OCEAN
January 1774
INDIAN OCEAN
South Pole
January 1775
January 1773
South America
South Georgia
Nov '72 – Jan '74
Jan '74 – Jan '75
Jan '75 – March '75
SOUTH ATLANTIC OCEAN
March 1775
South Africa
November 1772

△ The track taken by *Resolution* around the world during Cook's second voyage of 1772–5, showing the closest points to the Antarctic continent reached in January 1773 and February 1774 before the ice forced Cook to turn north again.

◁ During the first push into the Antarctic Ocean, *Resolution*'s sailors cling desperately to the yards as they struggle to take in sail. Freezing winds aloft and bare hands ripped bloody on frozen canvas and ropes, resulted in a grim ordeal for the men – despite their warm **Fearnought jackets** and an extra shot of brandy each time they returned shivering to the deck.

south of the Equator. For this second voyage Cook was given two ships, *Resolution* and *Adventure*. Both were converted coal ships like *Endeavour*, but *Resolution* was bigger.

Cook was also given an important new aid to navigation, the Harrison-Kendall "Timekeeper." This was the first ship's **chronometer** that was consistent enough to time the distances sailed from day to day and make it possible to calculate the ship's east-west **longitude** with great accuracy.

Cook's second voyage lasted from July 13, 1772 to July 30, 1775, and marks the beginning of Antarctic exploration. After the Antarctic Circle was crossed for the first time in January 1773, Cook's sailors had to endure incredible cold on the deck as the ships dodged floating icebergs and pack ice. Boat crews sent off from the ships to chip samples from the "ice islands," found that icebergs had one use: they were a useful source of fresh water. Though Cook sailed to within 120 km (75 mi) of the Antarctic mainland, pack-ice stretching out to sea prevented him from sighting the world's "last continent." This, the first voyage ever made around Antarctica, finally proved that no rich *Terra Australis* existed outside the southern polar seas.

During the winter Cook steered north into the warm Pacific to re-stock with fresh food and rest his men at New Zealand and Tahiti, discovering many more islands and island groups. Once again, he came home from this historic voyage of exploration without losing a single man to scurvy, although 31 men died from an infection caught when they visited an island.

19

▷ The track followed by *Resolution* and *Discovery* on Cook's third voyage, from Tahiti to the northwest Pacific coast of America. New discoveries on this voyage were Christmas Island and the Hawaiian Islands.

AFRICA

Cape Town
December 1776

Kerguelen Island
24 December 1776

AUSTRALIA

Tasmania

26 January
1777

NEW ZEALAND
12 February 1777

Hawaiian Islands
20 January 1778

10 June 1777
Tonga

TAHITI
13 August
1777

Worshipped as a god

By 1775 Cook's two voyages had added more detail to the map of the Pacific than all the voyages of the previous 150 years put together. The hard facts he had brought back had blown away all the dreams of finding a rich new continent in the southern Pacific. But another long-standing dream remained: the hope of finding a "Northwest Passage" around North America, linking the Atlantic Ocean to the Pacific. It was in order to find the Pacific entrance to such a passage – if one existed at all – that Cook's third and last expedition sailed from Plymouth on July 12, 1776.

Cook was now 47 years old and held the rank of captain. Once again he was given two ships: *Resolution*, and the small Whitby coal ship *Discovery*, commanded by Charles Clerke, who had sailed with Cook on his first two voyages.

As on his second voyage, Cook sailed for the Pacific via the Cape of Good Hope and Tasmania, revisiting New Zealand and using Tahiti as his Pacific base. From Tahiti he would cross the North Pacific to "New Albion": the California coast near modern San Francisco visited by Francis Drake on his round-the-world voyage in 1577–1580. This would be the starting point for Cook's search for the Northwest Passage.

The outward voyage was repeatedly delayed by damage to the ships – leaks and falling spars – caused by bad dockyard work in England. Cook did not reach Tahiti until August 1777, which meant he was too late to explore the North American coast that year. Sailing from Tahiti on December 7, the ships crossed the equator and on December 24, discovered the barren **atoll** of Christmas Island.

After 16 days' sailing north from Christmas Island, the ships sighted the Hawaiian islands of Oahu, Kauai, and Niihau. The islanders were friendly and spoke a language very like that of Tahiti. But when Cook landed on January 20, 1778, he was astonished when the islanders fell on their faces before him – a tribute to Cook indeed, for this was the salute paid by Hawaiians only to their god-kings (*ali'i'ai moku*).

◁ As Cook lands on the Hawaiian island of Kauai he is astonished when the islanders bowed deeply before him: a salute showing deep respect and submission.

△ Many new bird species sighted during the voyage were painted by William Ellis, surgeon's mate in *Discovery*. Among them was the Hawaiian Flycatcher.

21

Off Alaska's coast

Cook's first visit to the Hawaiian Islands lasted two weeks, long enough to take on fresh stocks of food and water. On February 2, 1778 he sailed for America to begin the search for the Northwest Passage.

A five-week voyage ended with the sighting of the American coast on March 7, but three weeks of bad weather forced Cook to search for a safe anchorage at which *Resolution*'s masts and rigging could be repaired. This he found at Nootka Sound, on the west coast of Vancouver Island, and on April 26, the exploration of the northwest coast began in earnest.

After a month of sailing along the mountainous, beautiful coast of modern British Columbia and southern Alaska, it was a disappointment to find the coast swinging west and southwest, ending in a long string of volcanic islands: the Aleutian Islands, where the English sailors met a party of friendly fur traders from Russia.

Once past the Aleutians, Cook followed the bays and inlets of the Alaskan coast until, on August 9, 1778, he reached the Bering Strait between Asia and America, "the Western extremity of all America hitherto known," he noted. For a few days the sea to the north of the Strait lay open, until at last, on August 17, the barrier of the northern ice blocked all further progress.

Determined to try again in the following year, Cook now steered for the Hawaiian Islands to rest his crews and repair his ships.

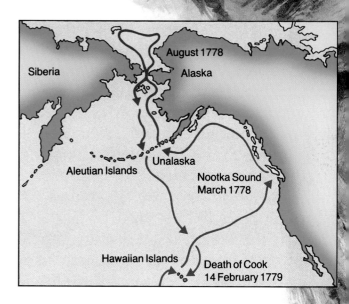

Siberia · August 1778 · Alaska · Aleutian Islands · Unalaska · Nootka Sound March 1778 · Hawaiian Islands · Death of Cook 14 February 1779

△ Cook's exploration of America's northwest coast in ice-free seas (March-August 1778).

▽ Halted by the Arctic ice – John Webber's drawing shows *Resolution* at the northernmost point reached by Cook (August 18, 1778).

▷ Off Alaska's icy coast, a boat's crew from *Resolution* hauls in a walrus they have shot. Though walrus oil and leather proved useful, even Cook could not persuade his men to eat the animal's meat, which proved unbearably tough.

Return to Hawaii

Retreating through the Bering Strait on September 2, Cook's ships paused for three weeks at Unalaska in the Aleutian Islands, making repairs before the long voyage south to the Hawaiian Islands. They sailed from the Aleutians on 26 October and sighted the Hawaiian island of Maui one month later.

Before he returned to the Arctic in the summer of 1779, Cook was determined to explore the new island group which he had named the "Sandwich Islands" after Lord Sandwich, First Lord of the British Admiralty. But first Cook needed a safe anchorage for his ships, to serve as a base. His final choice was Kealakekua Bay on the west side of Hawaii, where *Resolution* and *Discovery* dropped anchor on January 17, 1779.

The welcome offered by the people of Hawaii was more than friendly. They believed that Cook was none other than their god, "Lono," whose magic canoes had come across the sea to visit the islanders and bless them with gifts. When Cook's ships anchored in Kealakekua Bay the islanders believed that their legends had come true, and solemnly hailed Cook,

△ John Webber's portrait of a Hawaiian Chief wearing the feather-covered helmet and cloak of the islands, which Cook had seen nowhere else in the Pacific. He wrote that the Hawaiians valued them so highly they would not trade them.

the leader, as "Lono."

To the islanders the visit of the "gods" was a wonderful thing, and Cook and his men were given all the fresh food for which they asked. But the Hawaiians did not understand why the gods were so mean with gifts – especially objects made of iron, which the islanders prized above all. They thus resorted to obtaining the iron objects for themselves.

Cook and his men had plenty of experience, on Tahiti and other Pacific islands, of the lengths to which the islanders would go to steal iron objects from visiting ships. Here at Hawaii, they even came swimming out with stone· chisels to dig the nails out of the ships' sides. As one of Cook's officers wrote, "they seemed when they desired to go away not to have any idea they were doing wrong."

Despite these and other attempts at theft, it was a friendly visit. Cook's men were able to repair the ships' sails and *Resolution*'s **rudder**, and by February 4, Cook was ready to set off on his planned voyage around the islands. But three days out from Hawaii the ships ran into gales which split *Resolution*'s foremast. There was nothing to do but return to Kealakekua Bay for more repairs. To the islanders, however, this early return of the gods proved far from welcome.

◁ Under cover of darkness, two Hawaiians creep up *Resolution*'s side, unseen by the marine sentry on deck. As in the South Pacific, Cook's men had to stay constantly alert to stop the islanders from stealing objects made of iron.

25

Death of a great explorer

The Hawaiians were far from pleased to see *Resolution* and *Discovery* return to Kealakekua Bay. The 200 men in the two ships had cleared out most of the islanders' food stocks on their first visit. Now they were back, and clearly intent on a long stay, the mood of the Hawaiians changed.

The islanders felt cheated. They had welcomed the strangers as gods, but they were not gods – they could die. (An old sailor, William Watman, had died of a stroke during Cook's first stay at Kealakekua and had been buried ashore.) From the moment Cook's ships returned on February 11, 1779, his men noticed that things were not as they had been.

As work began on the damaged mast, thefts began to increase. The tongs of the blacksmith were stolen, and were not given back until a Hawaiian had been given 40 lashes with the **cat-o'-nine-tails** as a warning. Stones were thrown at the men working ashore. And then, on the night of February 13, *Discovery*'s ship's **cutter** was stolen from its moorings.

This was a loss that Cook could not ignore. Boats like the stolen cutter were vital for exploration work in shallow waters, and it had to be recovered. Cook decided to try a trick that he had used before in the South Pacific: to persuade an important chief to board his ship, and hold him to ransom until the stolen property was given back.

On February 14, Cook went ashore with fourteen armed marines. One barrel of his **musket** was loaded with small pellets, the other with a bullet. His intention was to invite the local chief, Kalei'opu'u (known to the English as "Terreeaboo") to return with him to *Resolution*.

The plan nearly worked. Cook and the unsuspecting Kalei'opu'u were walking back to the shore when an armed warrior sprang before them. Cook fired, but his musket pellets failed to kill the man. Encouraged by this, the Hawaiians attacked. The marines fled, leaving Cook to be killed at the water's edge.

After Cook's death, Captain Charles Clarke of *Discovery* took command. He buried Cook's body at sea.

△ The best-known portrait of Cook, painted in 1776 by Nathaniel Dance, from London's National Maritime Museum.

▷ The marine escort panics and runs for the boat, leaving Cook to be clubbed by the angry Hawaiians on the shore.

The legacy of Captain Cook

Clerke made one further attempt on the Arctic passage. Once again, however, *Resolution* and *Discovery* were beaten by the ice, and Clerke died of disease as the ships headed for home. They finally anchored in the Thames on October 4, 1780, after an epic voyage which had lasted four years and three months.

In his three great voyages, Cook had added eastern Australia, New Zealand, scores of South Pacific islands, the Hawaiian Island group and the Alaskan coast to the map of the Pacific. "The Grand bounds of the four Quarters of the Globe are known," wrote one of his admiring officers, Lieutenant James King, "and one part of Geography is perfect." In only 11 years, Cook had pushed the frontiers of ocean exploration north to the Arctic and south to the "last continent" of Antarctica, of which Cook ranks as the first true explorer.

Cook will always be remembered as a great seaman. To keep his ships seaworthy and his crews healthy on voyages of three years or more was a great achievement. He was also an expert navigator, a skill all the more to be admired because so much of it was self-taught.

Though strict in discipline, Cook was never a tyrant. He respected the customs of the Pacific islanders, and was deeply

△ Omai, native of the Tahitian island of Huahine, who sailed to England in *Adventure* after Cook's second voyage. "Good day, King Tosh!" he greeted King George III, when presented at Court.

◁ Gentleman botanist Joseph Banks, who sailed with Cook in *Endeavour,* in Tahitian dress.

28

worried about the terrible effects on them of diseases carried from Europe; but this was one problem which even Cook could not solve.

Cook was also always willing to help the scientists who sailed with him to pursue their studies and collect specimens. Joseph Banks recorded 3,600 plant species of which 1,400 had never before been described or written about and over 1,000 animal species of which half had not been noted. Sydney Parkinson completed 1,300 drawings on the first voyage. No other ocean voyages of the age gathered so much knowledge about the people, plants and wildlife of the Pacific world.

△ Cook's voyage added much to scientific knowledge of the plant and animal life of the Pacific. This is one of the many paintings and drawings made by botanist Sydney Parkinson.

▽ John Webber's drawing of *Resolution* and *Discovery* in Nootka Sound, where masts and spars were replaced before the exploration of the Alaskan coast and Bering Strait in 1778.

△ A vital tool for the calculating east-west positions: the Harrison-Kendall chronometer or "Timekeeper," carried in *Resolution* on Cook's second and third voyages.

Glossary

Astronomer Scientist who studies space and the movement of heavenly bodies.

Atoll Ring-like tropical island built up from the seabed by coral growth.

Boom Long, wooden spar used to extend a ship's sail.

Botanist Scientist who studies plants, flowers and trees.

Cat-o'-nine-tails Whip of nine knotted strands, or "tails," joined to a handle, used by the British to punish

▽ Cook's three voyages: *Endeavour* (1768–71), *Resolution* and *Adventure* (1772–75), and *Resolution* and *Discovery* (1776–80). Only the first voyage entered the Pacific westward round Cape Horn; the other two went out via the Cape of Good Hope, heading for New Zealand.

offending sailors (not banned in the Royal Navy until 1879).

Chronometer Watch or clock, used to time sections of a long voyage and help pinpoint the ship's longitude.

Cutter Large ship's boat driven by 8 to 14 oars.

Equator Imaginary east-west line around Earth, midway between the North and South Poles ("Latitude Zero").

Fearnought jackets Warm coats issued to Cook's sailors on his second voyage, to cope with the freezing temperatures of the Antarctic seas.

Hemisphere Half the Earth, either north or south of the equator, or east

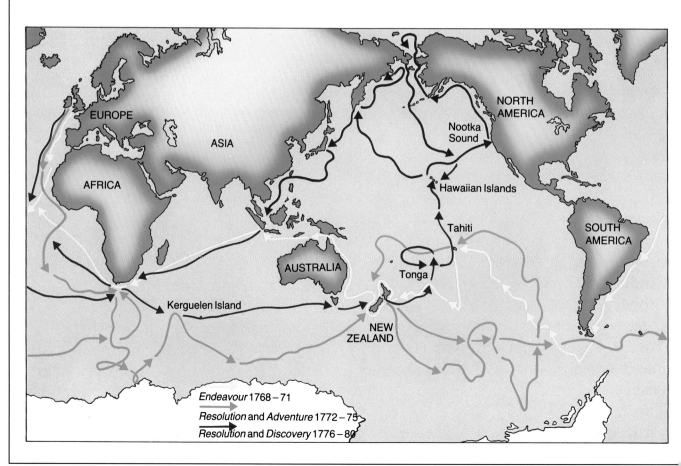

EUROPE · ASIA · AFRICA · NORTH AMERICA · Nootka Sound · Hawaiian Islands · Tahiti · SOUTH AMERICA · AUSTRALIA · Tonga · Kerguelen Island · NEW ZEALAND

Endeavour 1768 – 71
Resolution and *Adventure* 1772 – 75
Resolution and *Discovery* 1776 – 80

or west of "Longitude Zero."

Keel The lowest timber of a ship, from which the frames of the hull are built up.

Latitude A position north or south of the Equator, usually estimated by measuring the altitude of the sun at noon.

Longitude An east-west position, established on a voyage by measuring the distance and time traveled since the last known position.

Musket Long firearm with a smooth or unrifled barrel.

Rudder A flat structure hinged to the stern of a ship or boat for steering.

Navigation The act of directing a ship's movements and estimating its exact position at sea.

Natural scientists They sailed with Cook to collect and document species of plant and wildlife unknown to Europe. Artists made drawings and paintings as records of their findings.

Navigation The act of directing a ship's movements and estimating its exact position at sea.

Sounding The depth of water under a ship's keel, measured with a long pole or a weight on the end of a line.

Studding sails Small extra sails, supported by booms, used for extra speed in a favorable winds.

Yard Horizontal spar slung from the mast to which a ship's sail was fastened or "bent."

Yardarm Outer section and tip of a yard.

November 1520 – March 1521 First crossing of Pacific, by Ferdinand Magellan.

1579 Francis Drake discovers "New Albion" on California coast.

1605 – 6 Quiros and Torres discover New Guinea.

1612 – 40 Dutch seamen discover "New Holland" (western Australia).

1642 Abel Tasman discovers "Van Diemen's Land" (Tasmania) and sights New Zealand.

1728 Birth of James Cook.

1767 Cook sails for Tahiti in *Endeavour*.

June 1769 Transit of Venus observed on Tahiti.

October 1769 – March 1770 Cook explores and maps New Zealand's coastline.

June 1770 *Endeavour* nearly wrecked on Great Barrier Reef.

July 1771 *Endeavour* returns to England.

1772 – 75 Cook's second voyage, in *Resolution* and *Adventure*, completes the first voyage around Antarctica.

July 1776 American colonists declare independence from Britain; Cook sails on his third voyage, in *Resolution* and *Discovery*.

January 1778 Cook discovers Hawaiian Islands.

March – October 1778 Cook explores and maps Alaskan coast of northwest America as far as Bering Strait.

14 February 1779 Death of Cook at Kealakekua Bay, Hawaii.

Index

Adventure 19, 30, 31
Alaska 22, 28, 29, 31
Aleutian Islands 22, 24
America 4, 5, 21, 22, 31
Anson, Commodore George 10
Antarctic 19, 20, 28, 30, 31
Arctic 22, 24, 28
Asia 4, 5, 22
astronomer 9, 10, 13, 30
Atlantic Ocean 10, 17, 21
atoll 21, 30
Australia 9, 16, 17, 28, 31

Banks, Joseph 28, 29
Bering Strait 22, 24, 29, 31
boom 9, 30
botanist 13, 17, 28, 29, 30
Botany Bay 17
Britain 4, 5, 31
British Columbia 22

California 21, 31
Cape Horn 10, 30
Cape of Good Hope 17, 21, 30
cat-o'-nine-tails 26, 30
Christmas Island 21
chronometer 19, 29, 30
Clerke, Charles 21, 26, 28
cutter 26, 30

Dance, Nathaniel 26
de Bougainville, Chevalier 5
Discovery 21, 22, 24, 26, 28, 29, 30
Drake, Francis 21, 31

East Indies 16, 17
Endeavour 8, 9, 10, 13, 14, 15, 17, 18, 19, 30, 31
England 6, 14, 17, 21, 31
Equator 10, 14, 19, 21, 30, 31
Europe 4, 29, 31

fearnought jackets 19, 30

Great Barrier Reef 17, 31
Green, Charles 10, 13

Hawaiian Islands 21, 22, 24, 25, 26, 28, 31
hemisphere 4, 30

Kalei 'opu'u 26
Kealakekua Bay 24, 25, 26, 31
keel 8, 9, 31
King, Lieutenant James 28

latitude 18, 30, 31
London 6, 26
longitude 19, 30, 31

Magellan, Ferdinand 4, 5, 31
Maoris 14
Maritime Museum 26
Marton-in-Cleveland 5
Matavai Bay 13
musket 26, 31

natural scientists 9, 17, 31
navigation 4, 6, 19, 28, 31
Navy 6, 8, 30
New Albion 21, 31
New Guinea 5, 17, 31
New Holland 4, 15, 16, 31
New Zealand 4, 14, 15, 16, 19, 21, 28, 30, 31
Nootka Sound 22, 29
North Sea 6, 8
Northwest Passage 21, 22

Pacific Ocean 4, 5, 6, 10, 13, 19, 21, 28, 29, 30
Parkinson, Sydney 29
Pembroke 6
Plymouth 10, 21

Quiros 5, 31

Resolution 19, 20, 21, 22, 24, 25, 26, 28, 29, 30, 31
Royal Society 6, 13
rudder 25, 31

Sanderson, William 6
Sandwich Islands 24
Seven Years War 6
Solander, Daniel Carl 13
sounding 17, 31
South Pacific 5, 25, 26, 28
studding sails 10, 31

Tahiti 5, 6, 8, 10, 13, 14, 19, 21, 25, 31
Tasman, Abel 14, 16, 31
Tasmania 16, 21, 31
Tepau 13, 14
Terra Australis Incognita 4, 13, 14, 18, 19
Tierra del Fuego 10
Torres 5, 17, 31

Vancouver Island 22
Van Diemen's Land 4, 16, 31
Venus 6, 13, 14, 31

Walker, John 6
Wallis 5
Watman, William 26
Webber, John 22, 24, 29
Whitby 6, 8, 21

yard 9, 31
yardarm 17, 31
Young, Nicholas 14, 17
Young Nick's Head 14